Medieval World

The Life of a Knight

Kay Eastwood

Crabtree Publishing Company
www.crabtreebooks.com

Crabtree Publishing Company

www.crabtreebooks.com

Coordinating editor: Ellen Rodger

Series editor: Carrie Gleason

Designer and production coordinator: Rosie Gowsell

Scanning technician: Arlene Arch-Wilson

Art director: Rob MacGregor

Project development, editing, photo editing, and layout:
First Folio Resource Group, Inc.: Erinn Banting, Molly Bennett, Tom Dart, Jaimie Nathan, Debbie Smith, Aniko Szocs

Photo research: Maria DeCambra

Editing: Jocelyn Watt

Research: Susan Skivington

Consultants: Joseph Goering, Department of History, University of Toronto; Linda Northrup, Department of Near and Middle Eastern Civilizations, University of Toronto; David Waterhouse, Professor Emeritus of East Asian Studies, University of Toronto

Photographs: Alinari/Art Resource, NY: p. 12; Archivo Iconografico, S.A./Corbis/Magma: p. 14, p. 23 (bottom), p. 25 (right); Art Archive/Album/Joseph Martin: p. 10 (top left, bottom left); Art Archive/Biblioteca Comunale Palermo/Dagli Orti: p. 13 (right); Art Archive/Museo Civico Padua/Dagli Orti: cover, p. 4; Art Archive/University Library Heidelberg/Dagli Orti: p. 25 (left); Asian Art & Archaeology, Inc./Corbis/Magma: p. 29 (top right); With special authorization of the City of Bayeux / Bridgeman Art Library: p. 15; Bettman/Corbis/Magma: title page, p. 17 (right); Biblioteca Monasterio del Escorial, Madrid, Spain/Bridgeman Art Library: p. 27 (top); Bibliothèque Nationale, Paris, France/Bridgeman Art Library: p. 29 (bottom left); © Board of Trustees of the Armouries, Royal Armouries, London: p. 10 (right), p. 11 (top left), p. 11 (bottom left), p. 11 (bottom center), p. 11 (bottom right); British Library, London, UK/Bridgeman Art Library: p. 28 (bottom right); British Library/Cotton Nero E. II pt.2 f.220v: p. 7; British Library/Royal 14 E. IV f.210: p. 31 (bottom); British Library/Royal 14 E. IV f.244v: p. 6 (top); Centre Historique des Archives Nationales, Paris, France/Bridgeman Art Library: p. 29 (bottom right); Christie's Images/Corbis/Magma: p. 21 (top); Mary Evans Picture Library: p. 22, p. 26, p. 31 (top); Werner Forman/Art Resource, NY: p. 20; Giraudon/Art Resource, NY: p. 30; Glasgow Museums/Art Gallery & Museum, Kelvingrove/1939. 65e: p. 9; Master and Fellows of Corpus Christi College, Cambridge, CCC Ms 16, f. 85r (detail): p. 29 (top left); Maidstone Museum and Art Gallery, Kent, UK/Bridgeman Art Library: p. 21 (bottom); Musée de l'Armée, Paris, France / Giraudon/Bridgeman Art Library: p. 10 (center left); New York Public Library/Art Resource, NY: p. 13 (left); North Wind Picture Archives: p. 8 (top), p. 23 (top); Gianni Dagli Orti / Corbis / Magma: p. 28 (top); Private Collection/Stapleton Collection/Bridgeman Art Library: p. 11 (top right); Réunions des Musées Nationaux/Art Resource, NY: p. 11 (center right), p. 27 (bottom); Scala/Art Resource, NY: p. 17 (left), p. 28 (bottom left); Stapleton Collection, UK/Bridgeman Art Library: p. 16; Victoria & Albert Museum, London/Art Resource, NY: p. 24; K.M. Westermann/Corbis/Magma: p. 18

Illustrations: Katherine Kantor: flags, title page (border), copyright page (bottom), p. 5 (bottom), p. 6 (left), p. 8 (bottom), p. 15 (box), p. 21 (box); Margaret Amy Reiach: borders, gold boxes, title page (illuminated letter), copyright page (top), contents page (all), pp. 4-5 (timeline), p. 5 (map), p. 5 (bottom), p. 6 (left), p. 7 (parchment), p. 19 (all), p. 32 (all)

Cover: Knights displayed their coats of arms on their shields.

Title page: Battling knights try to knock one another off their horse using a long, thin pole with a sharp point, called a lance.

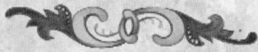

Crabtree Publishing Company

www.crabtreebooks.com   1-800-387-7650

Cataloging-in-Publication Data
Eastwood, Kay.
   The life of a knight / written by Kay Eastwood.
     p. cm. -- (Medieval world series)
   Summary: Describes the duties and privileges of a medieval knight in warfare and in service to a lord, and explores aspects of daily life such as clothing, apprenticeship, heraldry, and obedience to the chivalric code.
   ISBN 0-7787-1342-3 (RLB) -- ISBN 0-7787-1374-1 (PB)
1. Knights and knighthood--Juvenile literature. 2. Civilization, Medieval--Juvenile literature. [1. Knights and knighthood. 2. Middle Ages. 3. Civilization, Medieval.] I. Title. II. Series.
   CR4513.E25 2003
   940.1'088'355--dc22
                             2003016187
                                 LC

Published in the United States
PMB 16A
350 Fifth Ave.,
Suite 3308
New York, NY
10118

Published in Canada
616 Welland Ave.,
St. Catharines,
Ontario, Canada
L2M 5V6

Published in the United Kingdom
73 Lime Walk,
Headington,
Oxford
0X3 7AD
United Kingdom

Published in Australia
386 Mt. Alexander Rd.,
Ascot Vale (Melbourne)
V1C 3032

Table of Contents

The Middle Ages

Knights were powerful warriors on horseback who lived in a period of history now called the Middle Ages. The Middle Ages, or medieval period, lasted from about 500 A.D. to 1500 A.D. in western Europe.

During the Middle Ages, the most powerful people in society belonged to a ruling class called the nobility. The nobility included kings and lords. Nobles owned a lot of land, called a fief, and lived in **fortified** homes, called castles. They needed to protect their land from other nobles and from **invaders** from outside Europe who wanted more territory.

Knights fought for the nobles for 40 days a year in exchange for their own piece of land, called a manor. The knights swore an oath of loyalty to their **overlord**, becoming a vassal, or man of the lord. This system of exchanging land for protection is known as feudalism.

▲ *Knights rode expensive war horses called destriers. Stirrups, a Chinese invention which the Arabs introduced to Europe, and deep saddles, helped knights stay on their horses while fighting.*

Stirrups introduced in Europe; chain mail used for armor **750**	Knights charge with lances **1050**	Crusades to the Holy Land begin **1096**	Armor protects horses **1200**	Plate armor common; long swords popular **1300**

1000 Tournaments become popular	**1066** William of Normandy conquers England	**1150** Knights use coats of arms	**1250** Knights follow code of chivalry; rules of heraldry in place

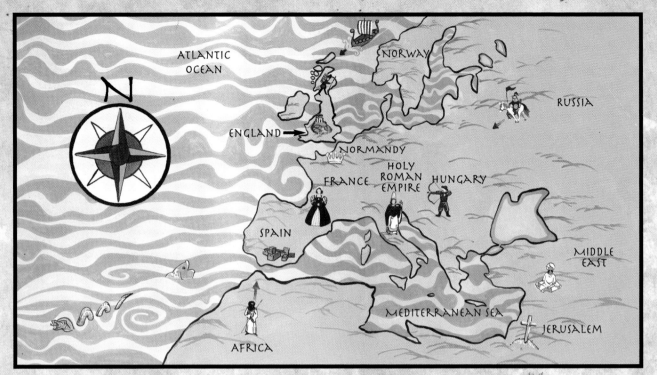

▲ *Western Europe in the Middle Ages looked much different than it does today. Most areas were ruled by kingdoms.*

People and Power

Most people in the Middle Ages were peasants who farmed the nobles' land. Even though they made up the majority of the population, they had the least power. Some peasants, called serfs, were not even allowed to move away from the land on which they lived without the lord's permission.

▶ *King*

▶ *Great lords*

▶ *Lesser nobles*

▶ *Knights*

▶ *Peasants*

Knights begin to use thrusting swords; introduction of longbows
1350

Knights no longer warriors, but landowners
1500

1320
Gunpowder introduced: first cannon used

1380
Archers replace knights as most important warriors; first handguns used

Becoming a Knight

A boy from a noble family went through a long period of training to learn how to fight and behave like a knight.

The Page

When he was about seven years old, a boy from a noble family moved to another noble's home to become a page. As a page, he learned good manners, how to follow orders, and how to carve meat properly and serve his lord at the dinner table. He ran errands, recited poetry, and entertained the ladies of the castle. Most importantly, the page learned how to use a small sword and ride a horse.

▼ *If a squire missed the quintain's target, a weight swung around and knocked the squire off his horse.*

The Squire

Around the age of fourteen, the page became a squire. The word "squire" comes from the French word *escuyer*, which means "shield carrier." One of the squire's jobs was carrying the shield of the knight who trained him into battle. The squire also looked after his knight's horse, armor, and weapons, and helped his knight put on armor.

In his spare time, the squire learned how to hunt, wrestle, and use large weapons. He also learned how to charge at an enemy on his horse by riding at full speed toward a quintain. A quintain was a target on top of a post. The squire had to hit the quintain with a long pole called a lance.

The Knight

Between the ages of 18 and 21, a squire became a knight. Usually, this happened in a ceremony called a dubbing that was performed by a squire's lord or by the king. The letter below shows how important becoming a knight was to a young man.

Dearest Elizabeth, my beloved sister,

I trust you are well. As you know, during the past month I turned eighteen. King Henry decided it was time for me to be made a knight. Let me tell you all about the ceremony.

First, I had to have my hair cut short to humble myself before God. I do not mean to dishonor our Lord, but I was sad to see my long curls hit the tiles. I then took a bath to wash away my sins. Afterward, my friends Stuart and John dressed me in a white linen robe to show the cleanliness of my body, a red cloak to remind me of my duty to shed blood while defending God, and black stockings, the color of death and the earth, to remind me that I will one day die.

Next, Stuart and John led me to the **chapel***. They left me alone for the whole night to pray. In the morning, they took me to the Great Hall. In front of Mother, Father, and all the people of the castle, King Henry dubbed me. I knelt before him and he tapped my shoulder with the flat side of his magnificent sword. Then, his other knights gave me my own sword and* **spurs***. I was officially a knight.*

Afterward, there was a large feast and I felt very important. I talked with William, one of the other knights, and he said that there was no time for such ceremony when he was dubbed. He was made a knight right on the battlefield, after a fierce battle. I hope I will be as brave in my first battle.

I hope that we will see each other soon.

Your loving brother,
Richard

A Knight's Armor

A knight's main job was to fight. To protect himself in battle, he needed sturdy armor.

The earliest knights wore armor made from tough cloth called linen that was stuffed with wool padding. When covered with wax or oil, it hardened and offered some protection against sword blows.

Wealthy knights wore waist-length shirts made of chain mail called hauberks. Chain mail was made from thousands of small iron rings linked together. It was strong and **flexible**.

By 1200, the hauberk reached to the knees. It was slit up the back and front so that the knight could walk and ride his horse. Some hauberks also had long sleeves and mittens to protect the knight's arms and hands. He also wore a hood, called a coif, to protect his neck, and leggings, called chausses, to protect his legs and feet. Under his hauberk, a knight wore a padded garment called an aketon. Aketons prevented swords from pushing chain mail rings into a knight's skin, cutting him, and causing an infection.

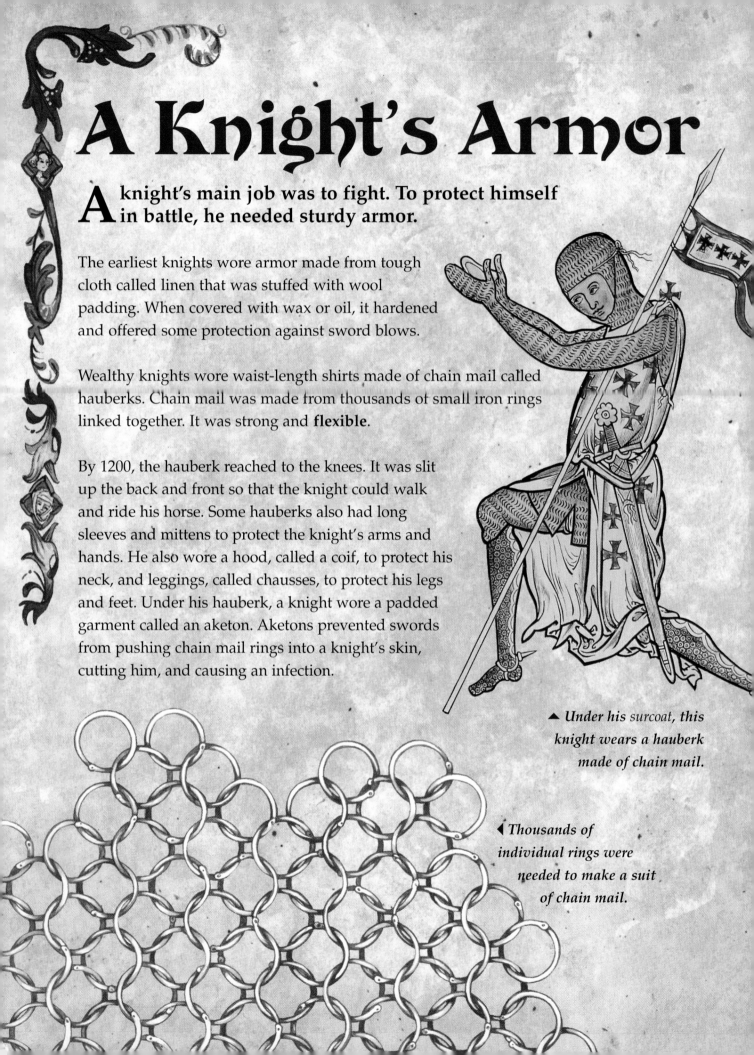

▲ *Under his surcoat, this knight wears a hauberk made of chain mail.*

◀ *Thousands of individual rings were needed to make a suit of chain mail.*

Plate Armor

In the 1300s, knights began to wear pieces of plate armor over their chain mail. The plates were made from iron or from leather hardened in boiling wax. Plate armor protected better against arrows, which pierced chain mail.

By the 1400s, wealthy knights wore full suits of plate armor. The armor was made of steel, which was much stronger than iron. A full suit of armor weighed between 50 and 60 pounds (23 and 27 kilograms) and had about fifteen pieces. Knights were very hot and sweaty in their plate armor since there were no openings to let in fresh air, except sometimes around the eyes and mouth.

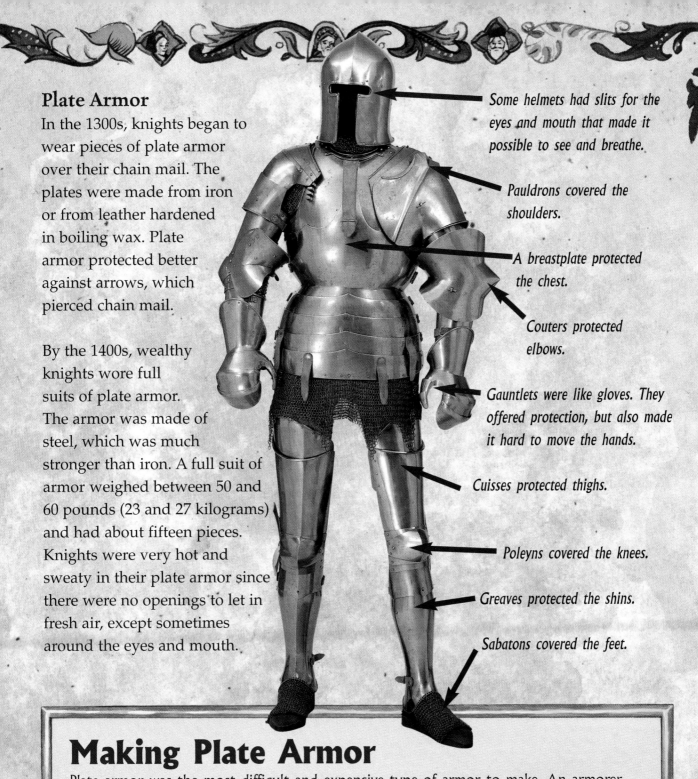

Some helmets had slits for the eyes and mouth that made it possible to see and breathe.

Pauldrons covered the shoulders.

A breastplate protected the chest.

Couters protected elbows.

Gauntlets were like gloves. They offered protection, but also made it hard to move the hands.

Cuisses protected thighs.

Poleyns covered the knees.

Greaves protected the shins.

Sabatons covered the feet.

Making Plate Armor

Plate armor was the most difficult and expensive type of armor to make. An armorer heated the metal to a very high temperature, then used a hammer to beat it into the proper shape for each plate. Once cool, he put the plates together on the knight to make sure they fit perfectly. The next step was to smooth and polish the plates, and join them together with tiny **rivets** and leather straps. A new set of armor was often dented because the armorer tested it by firing an arrow at it. The arrow dented a good suit of armor, but did not make a hole.

Weapons

The sword was a knight's most valuable weapon. Expert swordmakers made each sword out of the finest iron or steel, heating it, beating it into the right shape, and folding it many times to make it strong. A king or wealthy knight's sword was often decorated with gold and jewels. A good sword was a highly prized possession that a father passed on to his son.

Slashing Swords

Early swords were used to slash at enemies. Their wide, flat, two-edged iron blades were perfect for cutting off arms, legs, and heads.

Long Swords

Long swords became popular around 1300. They had longer blades than slashing swords and larger hilts, or handles, so that knights could hold them with two hands. Using both hands, knights added even more force to their blows.

Thrusting Swords

Thrusting swords, which were used after 1350, had sharp, narrow blades. Knights used them to pierce through the weak spots on plate armor, such as where the plates joined together. Thrusting swords were more difficult to use than slashing swords because knights had to aim them more carefully. By 1400, every knight had a slashing sword and a thrusting sword.

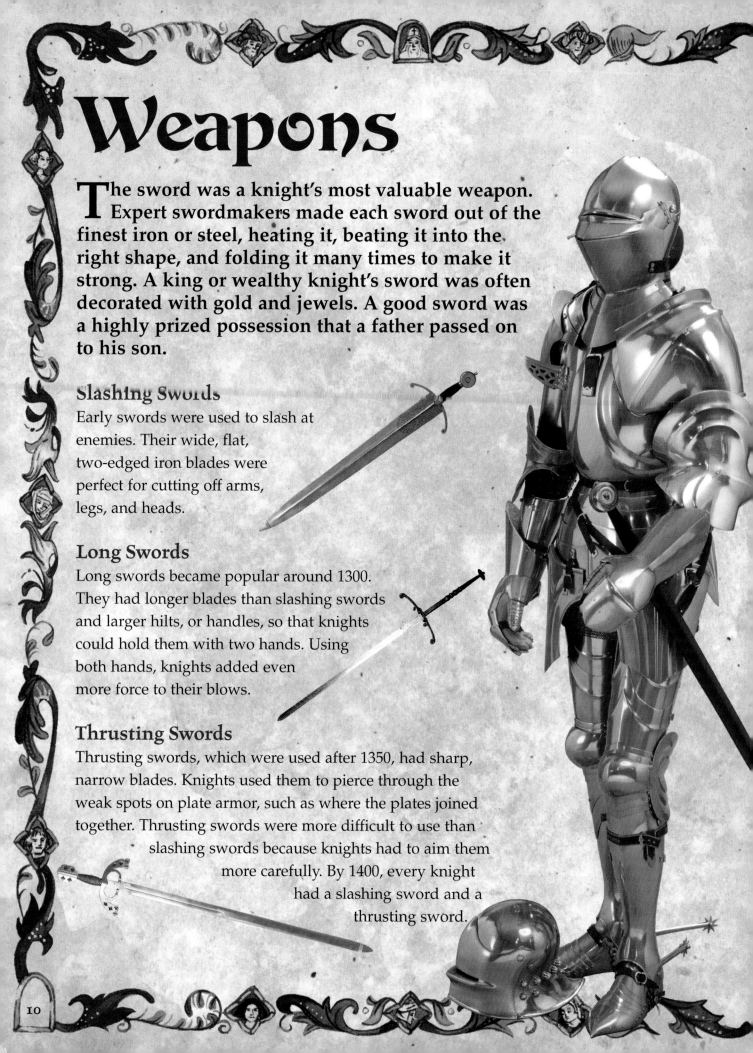

Other Weapons

Swords were not the only weapons that knights used when fighting. Some weapons had shorter handles, so they were easier to use in battles where there were a lot of people and horses in the way. Other weapons were better for smashing open armor.

◀ *Early lances were long, light, wooden poles with iron tips. Knights threw them at their enemies, like spears, hoping to pierce their chain mail. Later lances were longer and heavier. Knights charged at enemies with lances tucked under their right arms, using the lances to knock their enemies off their horses.*

▲ *Maces were used for smashing. A single blow with a mace could severely injure an enemy even if he was wearing armor.*

◀ *Knights used daggers when they fought on foot or when they broke or lost their swords. Daggers were good for piercing the joints of armor or stabbing enemies in the eye through the slits in their helmets' visors.*

◀ *A heavy iron battle-ax could cut a person in two.*

▲ *In the late Middle Ages, knights fighting on foot swung pole-axes to break open their enemies' armor. The blades were used for cutting, and the spikes for thrusting and hacking.*

▲ *The spikes on caltrops injured horses and people who stepped on them. No matter how a person threw a caltrop, it always landed with a spike pointing upward.*

Heraldry

Knights dressed in full armor all looked the same. To help them recognize one another in battle and prevent them from killing knights on their own side, they decorated their shields.

By 1150, knights and important noble families used specific designs and colors to identify themselves. These designs were called coats of arms, or arms, because they were sewn on the surcoats that covered knights' armor. Knights also painted their arms on shields and **banners** that they carried into battle, on buildings, and on **tombs**.

Over the next hundred years, less important knights and even squires chose coats of arms. A set of rules, known as heraldry, was put in place to make sure that only knights and nobles used arms and that no two knights or two families chose the same design.

Coats of arms were made up of many designs, including geometric shapes, plants, and animals. There were five main colors, or tinctures: blue, red, black, green, and purple. There were also two metals: silver and gold. Knights displayed their arms in a shield shape.

Heralds

By 1250, there were so many heraldic rules that experts, called heralds, kept track of them all. Since heralds could recognize knights by their arms, it became their job to carry messages to knights during battles and to identify knights who died. They also announced knights in pretend battles called tournaments.

Heralds kept a list of the coats of arms in a book called a registry. The registry showed and described each set of arms in great detail.

A Family's Arms

Members of the same family had similar coats of arms. For example, sons used their father's coat of arms with an extra symbol, such as a star, crescent, or moon shape. When a knight died, his eldest son took his father's coat of arms.

Daughters from very important families also had arms, especially if they were the only child. Women displayed arms in a diamond shape on banners, surcoats, and tombs. Girls used their fathers' arms until they married. Then, they kept their fathers' arms, took their husbands' arms, or combined the two.

A husband sometimes added his wife's arms to his own if she was from a powerful family. Their children then used the combined arms.

A herald decided what this coat of arms, which combines the arms of several important families, looked like.

Knights in Battle

A knight fought to protect his lord from enemies or to help his lord gain land. To gain another lord's land, knights and their armies marched to the enemy's castle and put it under siege. Castles were the stronghold of a lord's territory, and the place from which he ruled.

During a siege, the attacking army trapped the enemy, his family, and his household inside his castle and waited until the enemy's food ran out. In the meantime, the attackers used machines such as catapults and mangonels to throw enormous rocks and other objects at the castle walls. The defenders fought back, sometimes riding outside the castle to fight a short battle with the attacking knights.

Battles were also fought on battlefields at an arranged time and place. Knights were the most important warriors. Sitting on horseback, they charged at the enemy with great speed and force. Knights led armies of ordinary soldiers who fought on foot using daggers, **pikes**, pole-axes, and battle-axes.

▲ Knights and their armies fought in confusing battles called melees. Whichever side ran away first or suffered the most deaths lost the battle.

The Later Middle Ages

By the 1300s, highly skilled archers joined knights on the battlefield. They used longbow arrows to kill their enemies from far away. Eventually, archers became even more important than knights because their aim was so accurate and they did not need expensive horses or equipment, as knights did.

Warfare changed even more after cannon and guns were introduced in the 1300s. At first, these weapons were not very accurate and often injured the people who used them, but by the 1400s, they could kill many people from a distance. A knight's armor could not protect him from these weapons.

The Infantry

Unlike knights, foot soldiers did not owe a king or lord their services. Instead, the king or lord paid them to fight. Some foot soldiers were townspeople who could afford a weapon and some armor. Others were untrained peasants who were paid so little that they could not afford proper equipment.

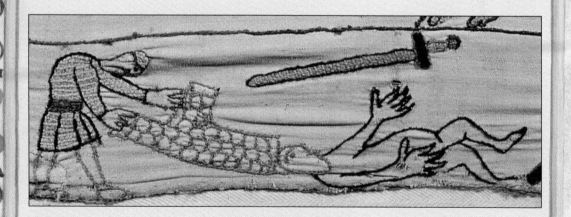

 *The Bayeux Tapestry is a large piece of embroidered fabric that shows the Battle of Hastings, fought in 1066. William the Conqueror, who was from Normandy, in present-day France, defeated the English King Harold II in a battle fought on English soil. In this section of the Bayeux Tapestry, poorer knights and foot soldiers take the weapons and armor of dead knights. This was often the only way they could arm themselves.*

The Crusades

Religion was a very important part of life in the Middle Ages. Christianity was the official religion of western Europe. Christians believe in one God and follow the teachings of his son on earth, Jesus Christ.

During the Middle Ages, Christians went on religious journeys called pilgrimages to the Holy Land. The Holy Land is the area that is now Israel, Jordan, Syria, and Lebanon. For Christians, Muslims, and Jews, the Holy Land is a place where important events in their religions occurred.

▲ *After the battle in which the Christians took Jerusalem, a holy city in present-day Israel, the streets were reported to have been knee-deep in blood because so many people were killed.*

Muslim Rule

Muslims, whom the Christians called Saracens, ruled the Holy Land during the Middle Ages. Muslims follow the religion of Islam. They believe in one God, whom they call Allah, and in the teachings of the **prophet** Muhammad.

In 1095, Pope Urban II, the head of the **Catholic** Church, called on Europeans to recapture the Holy Land from the Muslims. Over the next 200 years, kings and great lords traveled to the Holy Land with their armies of knights for a series of wars against the Muslims. These wars became known as the crusades and the people who fought them became known as crusaders.

▲ Christian warriors fighting for control of the Holy Land found it difficult to fight the Muslim warriors because they were not used to the area's hot, dry weather.

During the First Crusade, the Muslims were caught by surprise. The crusaders easily captured the holy city of Jerusalem and created small Christian kingdoms in the surrounding territory. Some knights stayed to rule and defend the kingdoms, but most returned home to their families.

There were seven more crusades to the Holy Land, but they were not as successful for the crusaders as the first. In 1291, the Muslims conquered the last Christian kingdom. Crusading in the Holy Land was over.

◀ In 1202, during the Fourth Crusade, the crusaders attacked the city of Zara, on the coast of the Adriatic Sea, near Italy.

Military Orders

Military orders were groups of knights who protected Christian holy places in the Holy Land. These warriors were different from regular knights because they were also religious men called monks.

Most monks lived in special communities called monasteries, where they spent their days praying and studying. The monks of the military orders did not live in monasteries. Instead, they fought against people who were considered enemies of Christianity. These monks believed that they were fighting as "soldiers of Christ."

Military orders stayed in the Holy Land to defend the new Christian kingdoms after regular knights went home to Europe. They built or took over many castles that still stand today.

▼ *Margat Castle is a crusader castle in present-day Syria that belonged to a military order called the Hospitallers.*

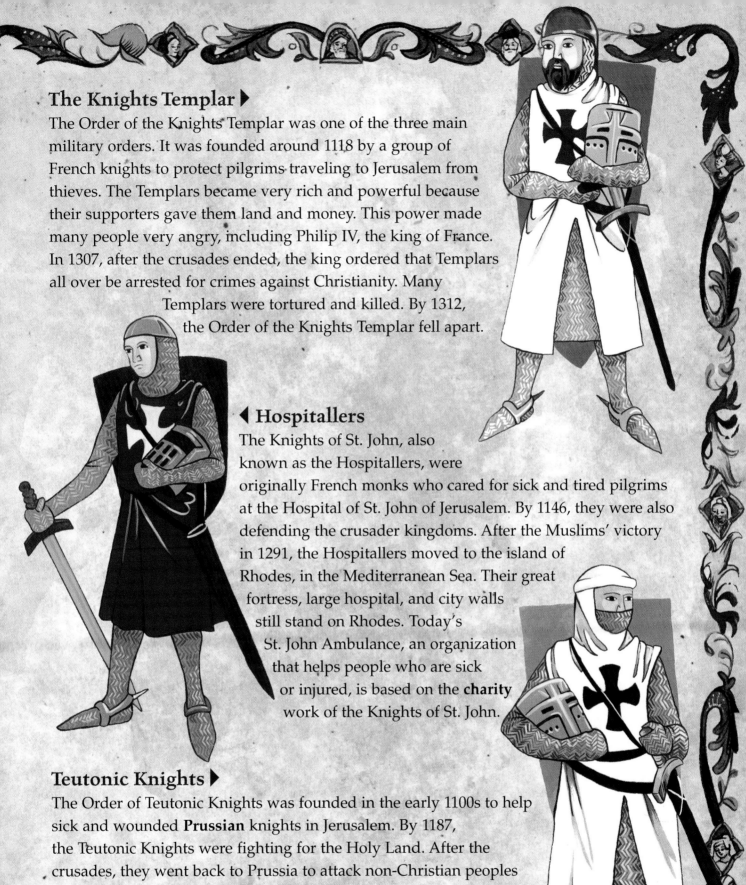

The Knights Templar ▶

The Order of the Knights Templar was one of the three main military orders. It was founded around 1118 by a group of French knights to protect pilgrims traveling to Jerusalem from thieves. The Templars became very rich and powerful because their supporters gave them land and money. This power made many people very angry, including Philip IV, the king of France. In 1307, after the crusades ended, the king ordered that Templars all over be arrested for crimes against Christianity. Many Templars were tortured and killed. By 1312, the Order of the Knights Templar fell apart.

◀ Hospitallers

The Knights of St. John, also known as the Hospitallers, were originally French monks who cared for sick and tired pilgrims at the Hospital of St. John of Jerusalem. By 1146, they were also defending the crusader kingdoms. After the Muslims' victory in 1291, the Hospitallers moved to the island of Rhodes, in the Mediterranean Sea. Their great fortress, large hospital, and city walls still stand on Rhodes. Today's St. John Ambulance, an organization that helps people who are sick or injured, is based on the **charity** work of the Knights of St. John.

Teutonic Knights ▶

The Order of Teutonic Knights was founded in the early 1100s to help sick and wounded **Prussian** knights in Jerusalem. By 1187, the Teutonic Knights were fighting for the Holy Land. After the crusades, they went back to Prussia to attack non-Christian peoples in northern Europe. The Teutonic Knights remained powerful through the 1300s, when northern Europe became Christian. The Order gradually fizzled out, but was formed again in Austria in the 1800s to do religious and charity work.

The Samurai

During the time of knights in western Europe, skilled fighters called samurai were waging war in Japan.

Samurai means "one who serves." The samurai pledged their loyalty to powerful **warlords** who fought one another for control of the countryside. In exchange for military service, samurai received parcels of land. Over time, the samurai became part of the ruling class. By the 1600s, when Japan was mostly at peace, many samurai lived in beautiful castles and followed a code of honor called *bushido*.

Samurai wore armor called *o-yoroi*. Plates of leather or iron were laced together with brightly colored silk. This beautiful armor was supposed to inspire samurai to perform great deeds in battle. The samurai also wore fierce facemasks called *mempo* to scare the enemy.

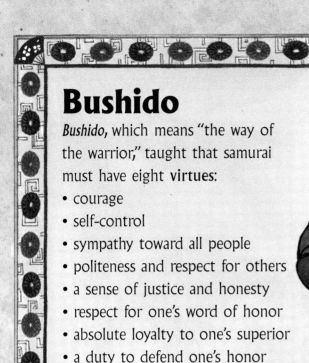

Bushido

Bushido, which means "the way of the warrior," taught that samurai must have eight **virtues**:

- courage
- self-control
- sympathy toward all people
- politeness and respect for others
- a sense of justice and honesty
- respect for one's word of honor
- absolute loyalty to one's superior
- a duty to defend one's honor

▲ *Unlike ordinary citizens, who had only one sword, the samurai carried two swords. The samurai often gave names to their swords because they believed that the swords had spirits or souls.*

A Samurai's Weapons

The samurai were expert fighters on horseback and on the ground. Early samurai fought with bows and arrows, but swords later became their main weapon. Swordtesters made sure that swords were sharp enough by making twenty cuts on the bodies of dead people or criminals waiting to be killed. They recorded the results, such as "one man cut in two" or "eight arms cut off," on the *nakago,* the metal piece that attached the sword blade to the handle.

Tournaments

Tournaments were an important part of a knight's life. These competitions began as a way for knights to stay in fighting form during times of peace. Tournaments were also a way for knights to make money to pay for their expensive weapons and horses.

During tournaments, two teams of knights fought mock battles, or melees, that lasted several days. The winners either took the losers' armor and horses, or kept the losers as prisoners and demanded a **ransom** for their release. The knight who performed best on the field usually received a prize.

Tournaments were supposed to be friendly, but they were often rough and disorderly. Many knights were injured or even killed. To make tournaments safer, the Church and kings encouraged one-on-one battles, such as jousting and sword fighting. The tips of weapons were blunted, or made less sharp, so that they were not as dangerous.

▲ *Lords and their wives, who were called ladies, watched melees from special boxes above the battlefield. In this painting from the 1400s, two teams wait for the signal to start the melee.*

Fun and Festivities

By 1200, most tournaments were enormous social outings for the castle community that lasted up to a week. Knights came from far and wide to show their skills and hopefully to earn a prize. Horse dealers, armorers, food sellers, storytellers, **minstrels**, and acrobats added to the festivities. There were also stone-throwing contests, wrestling matches, dice games, dances, and feasts.

Jousts

Jousts were contests between two mounted knights that were held in large, narrow arenas called lists. The goal of a joust was for one knight to knock his opponent off his horse by charging at him with a lance. The winner was the knight who stayed on his horse. If both knights stayed on their horse, the winner was the knight with the most points. A knight received points if his lance shattered when it hit his opponent's shield. He lost points if he missed hitting the other knight altogether, wounded his opponent's horse, or hit his opponent when the opponent's back was turned.

▼ *Ladies often served as judges at tournaments and awarded prizes, such as jewels and money, to the knights who performed best.*

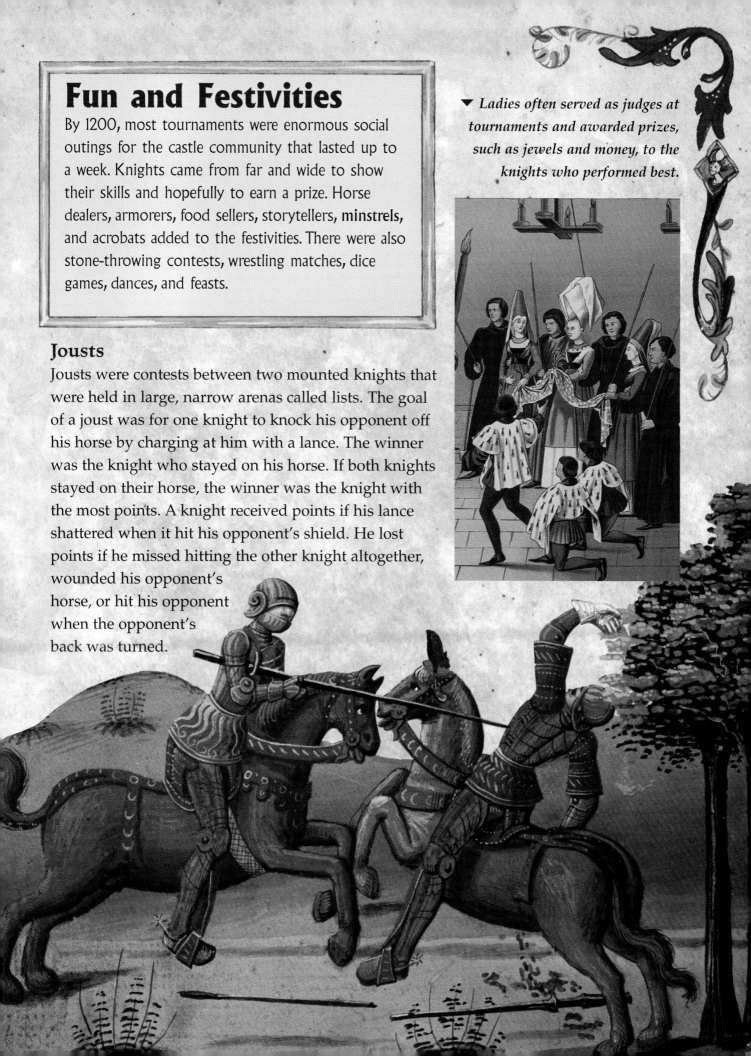

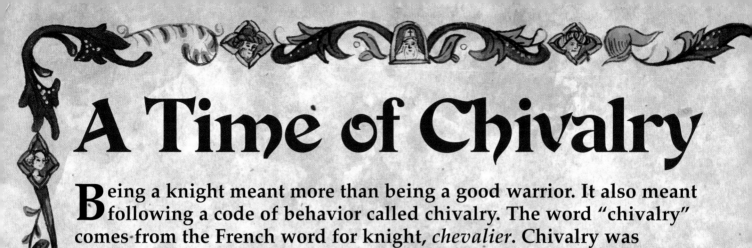

A Time of Chivalry

Being a knight meant more than being a good warrior. It also meant following a code of behavior called chivalry. The word "chivalry" comes from the French word for knight, *chevalier*. Chivalry was similar to *bushido*, the rules of honor that samurai followed.

The Beginnings of Chivalry

Early knights did not always behave properly. When there were no wars to fight, knights who did not own land fought one another, or attacked local peasants, stole their food, and burned their villages. The Christian Church tried to end this bullying around 1000 by introducing a set of rules which said knights were not supposed to attack women, peasants, or members of the Church who could not defend themselves. Knights were also not allowed to fight on religious holidays.

By 1250, when knights were part of the nobility, chivalry taught knights to be polite, never to swear, and to treat ladies well. The rules of chivalry also demanded that knights not kill other knights, especially knights who were not armed.

◀ *Knights found many ways to impress the ladies they loved, including taking them hunting on horseback. The ladies were often married to the knights' lords.*

A Knight's Code of Honor

A good knight should:

- defend his religion and protect the Church
- protect the weak, including women, widows, and orphans
- keep himself fit by exercising, hunting, and attending jousts and tournaments
- act in an honorable way
- show devotion to his lady
- never be satisfied with what he has done, but always wish to do more
- be brave, loyal, generous, polite, and honest, but never brag
- not attack an unarmed knight
- treat other knights well if they are taken prisoner and held for ransom

Learning About Chivalry

Pages and squires learned about chivalry at the home of their lord. They read or listened to stories about heroes, such as King Arthur and the Knights of the Round Table, who behaved as knights should. There were also instruction books that explained exactly how knights should behave. Knights everywhere were supposed to follow the rules of chivalry, but not all of them did.

▲ *Knights fought in tournaments in honor of their ladies, entertained their ladies with poetry, songs, and stories, and were supposed to treat them with great respect.*

◀ *Ladies often gave chaplets, which were circles of flowers they had picked in their gardens, to their favorite knights.*

Knights at Home

Knights did not spend all their time fighting in battles or competing in tournaments. When they were not fighting, knights made sure their manors were well managed, collected taxes from people on their land, and acted as judges in court cases.

▲ *Wealthy knights lived in large castles, while less wealthy knights lived in smaller manor houses. Everything a knight's family needed was inside the castle or manor's walls, including a chapel, stables, kennels, kitchens, storerooms, a bath house, a blacksmith shop, and an armory. The largest room in a knight's home was the Great Hall. It was the center of the household, where everyone ate and gathered for entertainment.*

A Knight's Family

Knights' families were usually large. There were so many illnesses and accidents that parents had many children. They wanted to make sure that at least one son lived until he was an adult so he could **inherit** his father's land. Mothers raised their young children with help from servants, who were usually girls from nearby villages or towns. At age seven or eight, the children were sent to other nobles' homes to learn how to be knights and ladies.

Finding a Bride

In the Middle Ages, knights rarely married for love. Instead, they tried to find rich wives who owned land so they could increase their own wealth. Kidnapping was one way to get a bride, even though it was illegal. Another way was to impress a king or great lord so much that he offered his daughter in marriage. In either case, women did not have much say in whom they married.

Having Fun

For entertainment, knights and their families listened to minstrels, who were musicians that traveled from castle to castle playing instruments, singing songs, telling stories, and sharing gossip and news. Knights and their families also played games, such as chess, and hunted deer, bears, wolves, and other wild game in the fields outside their castles or manor houses. They also trained hawks or falcons to hunt small birds and rabbits and bring the **prey** back to them. This was called hawking or falconry.

▲ *Musicians entertained guests at feasts, banquets, and other celebrations. In exchange for entertaining the castle inhabitants, they received food and a place to stay.*

▼ *Knights enjoyed playing chess because it was a good way to practice strategies that would help them win wars.*

Famous Warriors

Some knights were such good warriors and gained so much land and wealth that they became very famous. Warriors in other parts of the world also became famous for their skills in battle.

▼ Charlemagne (742–814)

Charlemagne was the greatest warrior king of the early Middle Ages. He made the area that is now France, Germany, and northern Italy a mighty Christian **empire**. In addition to being a courageous warrior, Charlemagne encouraged learning and the arts.

▼ Saladin (1137–1193)

Saladin was a Muslim ruler who led his army to an important victory against the crusaders at the Battle of Hattin, in 1187. Saladin then marched to Jerusalem and easily captured it from the Christians.

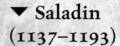

▲ El Cid, Rodrigo Díaz de Vivar (1043–1099)

Rodrigo Díaz, better known as El Cid, was a famous Spanish knight. He fought for both Christian kings and Muslim lords who controlled Spain. In 1094, El Cid's private army captured the Muslim city of Valencia, in eastern Spain. El Cid ruled Valencia until his death.

▼ William Marshall (1145–1219)

William Marshall was a wealthy, powerful English knight. His courage in battle impressed Eleanor of Aquitaine, the Queen of England, so much that she gave him the job of teaching her son how to be a good knight. When he was in his 70s, William advised another member of the royal family, King Henry III, who was only nine years old.

▼ Genghis Khan (1167–1227)

The great warrior Genghis Khan was born in Mongolia, in northern China. He created one of the greatest armies in the world. By the time of his death, he had conquered an enormous territory that included Central Asia, much of eastern Europe, and Russia.

◀ Minamoto Yoshiie (1041–1108)

Minamoto Yoshiie was a samurai who helped the Minamoto family become the most powerful family in Japan. His bravery earned him the nickname "Hachimantaro," or "First son of Hachiman," the god of war.

▲ Joan of Arc (1412–1431)

In the Middle Ages, women were not allowed to be knights. Sometimes, they defended their castles when their husbands were away, but they did not usually fight in battles. Joan of Arc is one exception. Joan was a young French girl who grew up during the Hundred Years War between England and France. Dressed as a man, she led the French army to many victories.

The End of an Age

Knights became less important as archers replaced them on the battlefield and as cannon and guns became common in battle. By 1500, most knights lived peacefully on their manors. They ruled their peasants, kept law and order, and only fought when they had to protect their families.

Mercenaries

Professional fighters, called mercenaries, also became important on the battlefield in the late Middle Ages, when wars began to last for months or even years. Mercenaries and their armies fought for as long as they were needed, not just the 40 days that knights owed their lords. They hired themselves out to the nobles who paid them the most.

▲ *Toward the end of the Middle Ages, knights were fighting less, so they had more time to take care of their manors and the people who lived on them.*

Knightly Orders

Knights were no longer valued as warriors, but the ideas of knighthood and chivalry remained important to nobles. Tournaments were still extremely popular events where nobles displayed their fighting skills and gathered to be entertained. Many knightly orders were formed to encourage the ideas of chivalry and nobility. Even today there are knights, although they no longer fight. People in England are still knighted for having accomplished great things.

▲ *Knights organized gatherings at their castles, with music, dancing, and feasting. Nobles from other areas traveled long distances for these gatherings.*

▼ *Unlike knights, mercenaries wanted money and valuable goods, not honor and glory. They fought in wars as full-time jobs, wherever they could be hired.*

Glossary

Arab A member of one of the Arabic-speaking peoples of the Middle East and northern Africa

banner A flag or other piece of cloth with a design on it

blacksmith A person who makes tools from iron

Catholic Relating to the Catholic religion, a denomination of Christianity

chapel A building or room for religious worship

charity The giving of help to people who are sick or in need

embroidered Decorated with a design sewn in thread

empire A group of countries or territories under one ruler or government

flexible Easily bent and not stiff

fortified Protected or strengthened against attacks

inherit To receive something from someone who has died

invader A person who enters using force

minstrel A person who entertains by singing or reciting poetry

overlord A lord who rules over other lords

pike A weapon with a pointed steel head, connected to a long wooden pole

prey An animal that is hunted by another animal for food

prophet A person believed to deliver messages from God

Prussian Belonging to Prussia, which was a state in what is now Germany and Poland

ransom A sum of money demanded in exchange for a prisoner

rivet A metal bolt that joins together other pieces of metal

spur A sharp piece of metal worn on the heel of a horseback rider's boots, used to make a horse go faster

surcoat A loose coat worn over armor

tomb A grave

virtue A valuable quality

warlord A military leader who controls an area of a country

Index

2 3 4 5 6 7 8 9 0 Printed in the U.S.A. 8 7 6 5